THE LEWIS AND CLARK EXPEDITION

SALLY SENZELL ISAACS

Heinemann Library
Chicago, Illinois

© 2004 Heinemann Library
a division of Reed Elsevier Inc.
Chicago, Illinois

Customer Service 888-454-2279

Visit our website at www.heinemannlibrary.com

Produced for Heinemann Library by
  Bender Richardson White.
Editor: Lionel Bender
Designer and Page Makeup: Ben White
Picture Researcher: Cathy Stastny
Production Controller: Kim Richardson

07 06 05 04
10 9 8 7 6 5 4 3 2

Printed and bound by Lake Book Manufacturing, Inc.

Library of Congress Cataloging-in-Publication Data.
Isaacs, Sally Senzell, 1950-
    The Lewis and Clark Expedition / Sally Senzell Isaacs.
       p. cm.--(The American adventure)
    Includes bibliographical references (p.   ) and index.
    Contents: Can we row to the Pacific?--Buying Louisiana--The great journey begins--Meeting American Indians--Winter at Camp Mandan--Journey into the unknown--Into the Rocky Mountains--Other side of the mountains--The ocean in view--Heading for home--Sharing the adventure.
       ISBN 1-4034-2503-5 – ISBN 1-4034-4774-8 (pbk.)
    1. Lewis and Clark Expedition (1804-1806)--Juvenile literature. 2. West (U.S.)--Discovery and exploration--Juvenile literature. 3. West (U.S.)--Description and travel--Juvenile literature. [1. Lewis and Clark Expedition (1804-1806) 2. West (U.S.)--Discovery and exploration.]
    I. Title.
F592.7.I83 2003
917.804'2-dc21

                                    2003005591

Special thanks to Mike Carpenter and Geof Knight at Heinemann Library for editorial and design guidance and direction.

Acknowledgments
The producers and publishers are grateful to the following for permission to reproduce copyright material:
Corbis Images/David Muench, page 25. National Maritime Museum, London/Ministry of Defence Archive, page 6. North Wind Pictures, pages 11, 13, 17, 20, 23. Peter Newark's American Pictures, pages 8, 14, 19, 26.

Illustrations by John James
Maps by Stefan Chabluk
Cover art by John James

Every effort has been made to contact copyright holders of any material reproduced in this book. Omissions will be rectified in subsequent printings if notice is given to the publisher.

QUOTATIONS
The quotations in this book come from:

Bakeless, John (editor), *The Journals of Lewis and Clark*. New York: Penguin Books U.S.A., Inc., 1964.

Ambrose, Stephen E., *Undaunted Courage: Meriwether Lewis, Thomas Jefferson, and the Opening of the American West*. New York: Simon & Schuster, 1995.

Ambose, Stephen E. *Lewis and Clark Voyage of Discovery*. Washington, D.C.: National Geographic Society, 1998.

The Author
Sally Senzell Isaacs is a professional writer and editor of nonfiction books for children. She graduated from Indiana University, earning a B.S. degree in Education with majors in American History and Sociology. She is the author of the nine titles in the *America in the Time of...* series published by Heinemann Library and of the first sixteen titles in Heinemann Library's *Picture the Past* series. Sally Senzell Isaacs lives in New Jersey with her husband and two children.

The Consultant
Our thanks to Laurie Heupel of the Lewis and Clark National Historic Trail Office, National Park Service, for her comments in the preparation of this book.

Note to the Reader
Some words are shown in bold, like **this.**
You can find out what they mean by looking in the glossary on page 30.

ABOUT THIS BOOK

This book is about the Lewis and Clark **Expedition** of 1804 to 1806 and other events in America surrounding it. An expedition is a journey made for a specific purpose, such as exploring. The term *America* means the United States of America (also called the U.S.)

Although the expedition took place long before there were telephones, cameras, television reporters, computers, or even typewriters, it is one of the best-documented events of United States history. Both Lewis and Clark wrote in journals. So did many of the men who traveled with them. This book contains some pictures and passages from these journals. Copies of the journals are in most libraries for you to read.

You will notice that many words from the journals are misspelled. In 1804, there was no dictionary of standard spelling, so people spelled words differently.

CONTENTS

ABOUT THE SERIES

The **American Adventure** is a series of books about important events that shaped the United States of America. Each book focuses on one event. While learning about the event, the reader will also learn how the people and places of the time influenced the nation's future. The little illustrations at the top left of each two-page article are a symbol of the times. They are identified in the Contents on page 3.

▼ This map shows the United States today, with the **borders** and names of all the states. Refer to this map, or to the one on pages 28 and 29, to locate places talked about in this book.

AMERICA'S STORY

Throughout the book, the yellow panels showing Jefferson's Peace and Friendship Medal contain information that tells the more general history of the United States of America.

THE FEATURE STORY

The green panels, showing William Clark's leatherbound journal, contain more detailed information about the Lewis and Clark **expedition,** this book's feature event.

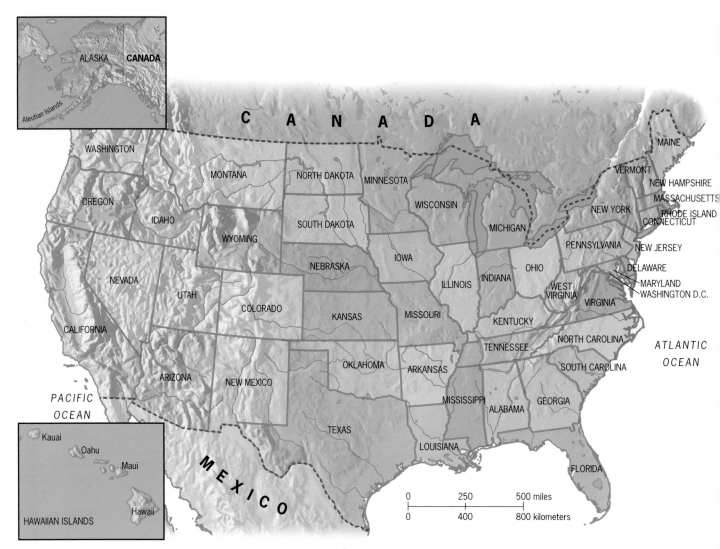

ALASKA **CANADA**

Aleutian Islands

WASHINGTON

OREGON

IDAHO

MONTANA

NORTH DAKOTA

MINNESOTA

WISCONSIN

SOUTH DAKOTA

WYOMING

MICHIGAN

NEBRASKA

IOWA

NEVADA

UTAH

COLORADO

ILLINOIS

INDIANA

OHIO

CALIFORNIA

KANSAS

MISSOURI

KENTUCKY

WEST VIRGINIA

VIRGINIA

MAINE

VERMONT

NEW HAMPSHIRE

MASSACHUSETTS

NEW YORK

RHODE ISLAND

CONNECTICUT

PENNSYLVANIA

NEW JERSEY

DELAWARE

MARYLAND

WASHINGTON D.C.

NORTH CAROLINA

TENNESSEE

SOUTH CAROLINA

ARIZONA

NEW MEXICO

OKLAHOMA

ARKANSAS

MISSISSIPPI

ALABAMA

GEORGIA

TEXAS

LOUISIANA

FLORIDA

C A N A D A

M E X I C O

PACIFIC OCEAN

ATLANTIC OCEAN

Kauai

Oahu

Maui

Hawaii

HAWAIIAN ISLANDS

0	250	500 miles
0	400	800 kilometers

THE LEWIS AND CLARK EXPEDITION: INTRODUCTION

Lewis and Clark became famous explorers in the early 1800s. What was the United States of America like at that time? Most adults had lived through the Revolutionary War and remembered the very first Fourth of July celebration. Only one third of the continent, from the Atlantic Ocean to the Mississippi River, belonged to the United States. France and Great Britain claimed much of the nothern part of the continent and Spain claimed much of the western and southern parts. Thousands of American Indians lived on much of the land. Most of the 5 million people in the United States lived within 50 miles (80 kilometers) of the Atlantic Ocean.

Even before he became the third president of the United States, Thomas Jefferson was not satisfied with a nation that took up a tiny part of the continent. He wanted the country to stretch into the vast open spaces of the West. Although there were no detailed maps of the continent, Jefferson had heard about the western land from explorers and **traders** of the Mississippi River and far-off Oregon. He heard that the land had rivers, mountains, wild deer, beaver, and buffalo, and thousands of American Indians.

Jefferson wanted the western land to become part of the United States. American farmers could use the land to grow food. Fur **trappers** could hunt there. Farmers and traders could use the seacoast at the Pacific Ocean and Gulf of Mexico to ship their goods to cities in Europe and Asia. All this was Jefferson's dream. To make the dream come true, he needed more details about the West. That was the mission of Meriwether Lewis and William Clark. As you read this book, use the map on pages 28 and 29 to follow the expedition of Lewis and Clark.

A ROUTE TO THE PACIFIC?

President Jefferson dreamed of a nation that stretched from the Atlantic Ocean to the Pacific Ocean. But first, Americans needed to get to the Pacific Ocean. There were no roads or railroad tracks. There were just rivers. No one knew whether it was possible to follow the rivers across the continent from one ocean to the other.

In 1792, the United States reached only to the Mississippi River. In the southern states, such as Virginia, the Carolinas, and Georgia, there were many large farms, called **plantations.** Most of the work was done by **slaves.** In the northern states, the nation's first cotton **mill** opened in Rhode Island in 1792. In the mill, machines turned cotton into yarn. This was the first of many mills and factories in northern states.

From 1787 to 1800, the United States grew from thirteen to sixteen states. In 1800, the population was about one-fiftieth of what it is today. About 5 million people lived in the United States. Nearly 900,000 of them were slaves.

THE FUR TRADE
Fur trading was an important business. Trappers, many of them American Indians, combed the forests for beavers and the oceans for sea otters.

At **trading posts, trappers** met **traders** who exchanged rifles, knives, and kettles for furs. Traders sent the furs by ship to Europe and China, where they were traded for valuable tea, silk, and chinaware. Fur hats and coats were quite fashionable and expensive.

If the United States could control land in the West and along the oceans, it would help the nation's fur-trading business.

▲ Great Britain sent Captain James Cook to find a water route from the Atlantic to the Pacific Ocean. In 1778, Cook sailed into present-day Vancouver Island in western Canada. American Indians in their canoes surrounded the **British** ships.

From sea to sea

In 1800, Thomas Jefferson became the third president of the United States. For years, Jefferson had read about the fur trappers and traders from the United States, France, and Great Britain who scouted the forests in land west of the Mississippi River for valuable animal furs. Jefferson knew that Great Britain had set up trading posts in the far western Oregon Country. He knew that British explorers were in Canada searching for a way to cross North America from the Atlantic to the Pacific oceans. In 1800, Jefferson read that the Englishman Alexander Mackenzie finally found a way. When Jefferson learned this news, he grew worried. What if Great Britain took over Oregon, California, and the rest of the West?

▼ In 1792, the United States sent Robert Gray from Boston southward around Cape Horn, and up the Pacific coast to a river in Oregon Country. He named the river after his ship, *Columbia*. Gray's report helped Lewis and Clark reach the Pacific.

◀ Chinook Indians lived by the Columbia River when Robert Gray's ship sailed in. These people became experts at trading with Europeans. Many of them died, however, from diseases brought by the white traders.

FOR THE PEOPLE

Thomas Jefferson felt the government should not interfere in people's lives. He said he represented "the common man." (In those days, only white men could be United States citizens, with the right to own land and to vote. Women, slaves, and American Indians could not be citizens.) Jefferson's political party was called the Democratic-Republican Party. The other party, the Federalists, believed in a strong national government and a powerful president.

BUYING LOUISIANA

In 1802, the United States counted on the kindness of France for trade. The nation needed to use the port of New Orleans, on the Gulf of Mexico. New Orleans is in Louisiana. In 1802, Louisiana belonged to France.

Farmers from such places as Illinois and Kentucky sent their crops down the Mississippi River to the **port** at New Orleans. They shipped their goods from the Gulf of Mexico north to cities on the East Coast. Jefferson was afraid that France might one day stop the United States from using the port. He wanted the United States to control New Orleans. Jefferson sent Robert Livingston to France to offer over $9 million for New Orleans.

WHO WANTS LOUISIANA?
1682 French explorer LaSalle explores the land and names it after France's King Louis XIV.
1763 France loses the **French and Indian War** and gives part of the land to Britain and the rest to Spain.
1800 Spain gives Louisiana back to France in exchange for a small section of Italy.
1803 The United States buys Louisiana from France.

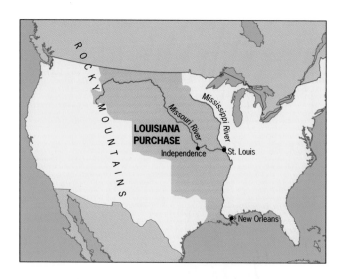

After much consideration, France's ruler, Napoleon Bonaparte, decided to sell all of Louisiana. He had no use for the American wilderness, and he needed the money for his French army to fight his wars with Great Britain in Europe. The two sides agreed to a price of $15 1/2 million. By adding Louisiana **Territory,** the United States doubled in size. Now when Jefferson sent explorers to the West, much of their **expedition** would be on United States land.

▲ Part or all of fifteen states were formed from the Louisiana Purchase, as can be seen by comparing this map with the one on page 4.

▶ No one consulted the American Indians about selling Louisiana. Many Sioux, Cheyenne, Shoshone, and other tribes had been living on the land for thousands of years.

8

Making plans

Even before the Louisiana Purchase, Jefferson was planning to send a group of explorers to the Pacific. Now he had even more reasons to learn about the West. Easteners knew very little about the land west of the Mississippi River.

Jefferson chose his personal secretary and friend, Meriwether Lewis, to lead the trip. The trip had many goals. The main ones were: to find a water route to the Pacific Ocean, to observe the Pacific fur trade of the **British,** to get to know the American Indians, to learn about the animals and plants of the West, and to make maps and gather information for United States settlers to move westward. Jefferson sent Lewis to the town of Philadelphia to meet with experts in the study of medicine, stars, mapmaking, plants, and American Indian history.

◀ This picture shows President Jefferson (sitting) and Meriwether Lewis at the White House.

MERIWETHER LEWIS
Lewis started school in Georgia. At thirteen, his mother sent him to Virginia to live in a teacher's home and get an education. At eighteen, Lewis took over running the family **plantation,** where his neighbor was Thomas Jefferson. Longing for adventure, Lewis joined the army, where he enjoyed horseback riding and canoeing in the wilderness.

THE JOURNEY BEGINS

Jefferson called the expedition "the Voyage of Discovery." There were so many mysteries about the West. Was the land good for farming? Were the American Indians friendly or warlike? Would the Rocky Mountains be too high to cross? Was there a continuous water route to the Pacific Ocean?

SUPPLIES

Lewis could only guess what supplies he would need for the trip. He brought a compass, a telescope, thermometers, and other instruments. Camping supplies included blankets, soap, candles, food, mosquito netting, and cloth for tents.

Gifts for the American Indians included 144 pocket mirrors, 4,600 sewing needles, 144 small scissors, 33 pounds of tiny beads, plus tobacco and pipes.

▼ The **expedition** started on the Missouri River. The crew traveled in one large **keelboat** and two **pirogues,** which are large canoes made from tree trunks. When the river was deep, the men rowed or sailed. When it was shallow, they struggled to push poles against the river bottom to move the boats forward. Sometimes the men had to wade to the muddy shore and pull the boats with ropes. All the while, they swatted at annoying mosquitoes.

Another leader

Lewis figured the trip would take about two years. Leading the expedition was a huge task. It was too risky to have just one leader. If something happened to him, another would need to take charge. Lewis chose William Clark. They had served in the army together for six months. Lewis knew that Clark was an honest man, an encouraging leader, and was better at boating and mapmaking than Lewis himself.

Choosing a crew

Over 100 men applied to join the Lewis and Clark expedition. The two captains wanted trustworthy men who were skilled builders, blacksmiths, boatmen, and hunters. The captains also chose a man named George Drouillard because he was an expert hunter and could speak English, French, and a few American Indian languages. Clark brought with him his **slave,** York, who had been his companion since childhood.

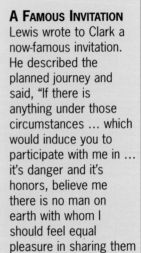

A FAMOUS INVITATION
Lewis wrote to Clark a now-famous invitation. He described the planned journey and said, "If there is anything under those circumstances … which would induce you to participate with me in … it's danger and it's honors, believe me there is no man on earth with whom I should feel equal pleasure in sharing them as with yourself."

Lewis brought with him his constant companion, a dog named Seaman. Though some men and one woman were added and others left the group along the way, about 35 people made the voyage from start to finish. These **expedition** members were called the Corps of Discovery. The corps spent the winter of 1803 training at Camp Dubois, located near St. Louis. At the time, it was one of the last **settlements** before the wilderness. The Lewis and Clark expedition finally began on May 14, 1804.

▲ An artist carved this picture in wood. The picture shows one of the boats stuck in the mud near the shore.

11

AMERICAN INDIANS

People are wrong when they say the West had no settlers in 1804. The Voyage of Discovery met 58 different American Indian tribes. President Jefferson had instructed Lewis to form friendships with the American Indians. In August 1804, this task began.

The corps was near present-day Omaha, Nebraska, on the **border** between Iowa and Nebraska. The men called the place Council Bluff. The captains sent Drouillard to find members of the Oto and Missouri tribes and bring them to a meeting. Drouillard returned with 12 men who said there were about 250 of their people living in the area. The Oto and Missouri had met white fur **traders** before. They liked trading with whites to get guns to fight their enemy tribes. But they also knew that white people carried deadly diseases, such as smallpox, which had already killed thousands of their people.

Lewis talks to the American Indians
Dressed in his army uniform, Lewis stood beside the United States flag and made a speech. He wanted to make the American Indians respect the United States and welcome the nation's traders to their land. He addressed his audience as "Children." He referred to President Jefferson as "your only great father." Lewis warned that if the American Indians angered the president, American traders would stop providing them with guns. Then he handed out small medals with Jefferson's picture, combs, paint, gunpowder, and whiskey. Lewis would repeat this performance for other tribes.

12

The Teton Sioux

The Oto and Missouri people were not especially impressed with the corps. But they were peaceful. Farther up the Missouri River, the Teton Sioux were not so peaceful. The Tetons were successful traders with other tribes. They did not want white traders in the area to spoil their business. When the corps arrived, one Teton chief, Black Buffalo, was friendly. He welcomed them with a feast of barbecued buffalo and roasted dog meat. But another chief, Partisan, tried to steal the **keelboat.**

MEETING AMERICAN INDIANS MAY TO OCTOBER 1804
(Present-day locations)
August 2 Oto and Missouri near Omaha, Nebraska
August 27 Yankton Sioux near Yankton, South Dakota
September 23 Teton Sioux near Pierre, South Dakota
October 8 Arikara in Standing Rock Indian **Reservation,** South Dakota
October 24 Mandan, Hidatsa, and Assiniboins near Bismarck, North Dakota

◀ Patrick Gass drew this picture of the meeting at Council Bluff between the American Indians and the corps. It took Lewis an hour and a half to give his speech. It took as long for Drouillard to translate Lewis's words into the Oto language. Lewis could not be sure that his words were understood.

◀ After the Corps of Discovery spent four days with the Teton Sioux, Chief Partisan sent his men to steal the keelboat. Lewis ordered his men to draw their guns. Two hundred Tetons ran to the shore with spears, bows and arrows, hatchets, and guns. They were prepared to fight to the death. Luckily, Chief Black Buffalo arrived and stopped Partisan's warriors.

DAILY DIARY
The boats covered about 10 to 30 miles (16 to 64 kilometers) a day. Here is a typical day on the move:
5:00 A.M. Wake up.
5:15 A.M. Pack up and gulp down leftovers from last night's dinner.
5:45 A.M. Start moving.
12:00 NOON Eat on the move.
5:00 P.M. Stop, hand out food, and cook it over an open fire. Often the men listened to fiddle music, sang, and danced. The captains watched the position of the stars and wrote in their journals.
10:00 P.M. Sleep out in the open with bear or deer robes for cover.

WINTER AT CAMP MANDAN

By the end of October, the corps had traveled more than four months and 1,600 miles (2,574 kilometers). They were near present-day Bismarck, North Dakota. Snow was falling. The comforts of home seemed far, far away. It was time to stop for the winter.

French fur **traders** had told Lewis and Clark about five villages belonging to the Mandan and Hidatsa tribes. It was an active area where French and English traders brought furs to exchange for guns and food. The Crow and Cheyenne tribes traded horses for corn and beans. The Sioux traded buffalo meat for tobacco and vegetables.

The corps met two French traders who lived with the American Indians. They helped **translate** Lewis and Clark's request to build a winter camp nearby. The Mandan welcomed them. One of the Frenchmen agreed to help guide the corps through the unknown land ahead. His name was Toussaint Charbonneau. One of his two wives, Sacagawea, was a Shoshone Indian. She could help communicate with her tribe, which lived farther west.

The corps built Fort Mandan in the shape of a triangle. Rows of log huts formed two sides. An 18 foot (5.5-meter)-high wall formed the other. It was a peaceful winter. Some of the explorers hunted buffalo with the Mandan. By February, though, food was scarce. Mandan and Hidatsa visitors came to the camp to examine such strange sights as the blacksmith's **bellows.** The blacksmith made axes and traded them with the Mandan visitors for corn.

▼ George Catlin painted this picture of the Mandan in a Buffalo Bull Dance. The Mandan believed the dance would bring buffalo to their land and bring skill to the buffalo hunters.

The picture shows the center of a Mandan village, which had 40 to 50 earthen lodges around an open area. Each lodge held a family of about ten people. Near the village, Mandan women grew beans, squash, corn and sunflowers. Men hunted deer, elk, and buffalo.

14

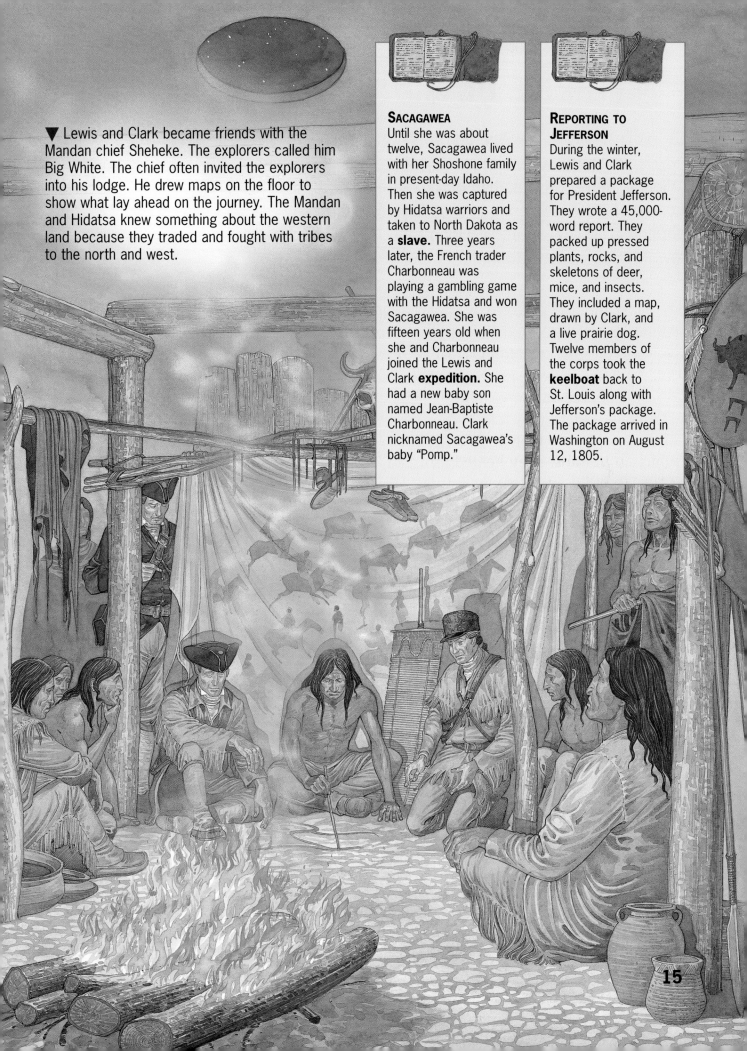

▼ Lewis and Clark became friends with the Mandan chief Sheheke. The explorers called him Big White. The chief often invited the explorers into his lodge. He drew maps on the floor to show what lay ahead on the journey. The Mandan and Hidatsa knew something about the western land because they traded and fought with tribes to the north and west.

SACAGAWEA

Until she was about twelve, Sacagawea lived with her Shoshone family in present-day Idaho. Then she was captured by Hidatsa warriors and taken to North Dakota as a **slave.** Three years later, the French trader Charbonneau was playing a gambling game with the Hidatsa and won Sacagawea. She was fifteen years old when she and Charbonneau joined the Lewis and Clark **expedition.** She had a new baby son named Jean-Baptiste Charbonneau. Clark nicknamed Sacagawea's baby "Pomp."

REPORTING TO JEFFERSON

During the winter, Lewis and Clark prepared a package for President Jefferson. They wrote a 45,000-word report. They packed up pressed plants, rocks, and skeletons of deer, mice, and insects. They included a map, drawn by Clark, and a live prairie dog. Twelve members of the corps took the **keelboat** back to St. Louis along with Jefferson's package. The package arrived in Washington on August 12, 1805.

15

INTO THE UNKNOWN

On April 7, 1805, Lewis wrote in his journal: "We were now about to penetrate a country at least two thousand miles in width, on which . . . civilized man had never trodden." Traveling in six new canoes and the two pirogues, the corps paddled along the Missouri River toward present-day Montana.

The Mandan had correctly predicted a fast-flowing river, plenty of buffalo, and the danger of grizzly bears. The corps followed the Mandan's instructions past the Yellowstone and Milk rivers. They next expected to see the Great Falls, which the Mandan had described. They were not prepared to see two rivers meeting at a **fork.** Which of these was the Missouri River? If the captains chose the wrong fork, the corps would lose valuable time getting to the Pacific. The group split-up to investigate. Lewis took one group up the north fork. Clark took another to the south. They returned after several days and compared notes. The captains agreed that the south fork seemed like the right direction. The entire corps sighed with relief when they finally heard the powerful thunder of the Great Falls.

Getting around the Great Falls

There was no way to take the boats and equipment over the falls. Everything had to be carried around them. This is called a **portage.** Only the canoes and part of the supplies would continue on the trip. The corps hid the two **pirogues** in the bushes. They buried food and the rest of the supplies underground. The corps would pick all these up on the return trip. To transport the remaining canoes and the supplies, the men chopped a huge cottonwood tree and built two wagons. They began the portage on June 22. It took thirteen days. The temperature was hot and the gnats and mosquitoes swarmed. The ground was covered with sharp stones and prickly cactus that tore through the men's moccasins. During a rainstorm, the corps was hit by hail the size of pigeons' eggs.

▶ It was an 18-mile (29-kilometer) trip around the Great Falls. The corps made the trip eleven times to transport the canoes and supplies.

THE JOURNEY SO FAR
May 14, 1804 Leave Camp Dubois
October 24 Arrive at Mandan and Hidatsa villages
November 4 Charbonneau and Sacagawea join the trip
April 7, 1805 Leave Fort Mandan
May 26 Lewis first sees the Rocky Mountains
June 22 Begin portage of Great Falls
July 4 Complete portage of Great Falls

16

Moving on

The corps had been carrying an iron frame to make a boat for this part of the trip. Lewis supervised the men as they put the frame together and covered it with elk and buffalo skins. Unfortunately, the trees in the area did not produce resin, a sticky material needed to seal the boat. At the start, the boat leaked badly. Lewis ordered the boat to be sunk. Clark ordered the men to build two more canoes. Then the journey continued.

◀ On June 5, 1805, Clark drew this picture of a sage grouse. It was one of the 122 animals that were unknown east of the Mississippi River. The other animals included coyotes, mountain goats, black-tailed prairie dogs, and grizzly bears. The **expedition** also found 178 new plants.

YORK

York was Clark's African-American **slave.** He was an excellent swimmer, hunter, and **trapper** who helped the Voyage of Discovery succeed. At the time, the U.S. government allowed people to own slaves. Virginia, Clark's home state, had more slaves than any other. When the expedition ended, York asked for his freedom so that he could live near his wife, a slave in Kentucky. About ten years later, Clark granted that freedom.

THE ROCKY MOUNTAINS

With the Great Falls behind them, the captains sensed that they were approaching the headwaters of the Missouri River near present-day Three Forks, Montana. They would soon learn that it was time to leave their canoes and try to get some horses.

Three rivers met to form the **headwaters** of the Missouri River. Lewis and Clark hoped that one of the rivers flowed into the Columbia River and out to the Pacific Ocean. But they had no such luck. They would have to cross the mountains on foot. They would need horses to carry their supplies. The men hid some of their supplies and sank their canoes in a pond. They hoped that they could pick them up on their return trip.

The land looked familiar to Sacagawea. This had been her home until five years ago when the Hidatsas captured her.

The Shoshone

At last, Lewis found some Shoshone. But because they had never seen a white man before, the Shoshone ran away. Finally some women led Lewis to their chief, Cameahwait. Later, when Sacagawea met the chief, she wept with joy. He was her brother.

Cameahwait described the mountain trail as nearly impossible to pass. Sacagawea **translated** this to Lewis and Clark. But the captains would not be discouraged. They traded some guns, handkerchiefs, knives, and trinkets with the Shoshone for 29 horses. On September 1, the group set off with a Shoshone guide named Toby on the most dangerous part of their journey.

For nearly three miserable weeks, the explorers plodded through snow that froze through their moccasins. They drank melted snow. Their food supplies were desperately low. To avoid starvation, they ate some of their horses.

▼ The corps spent nearly three weeks on the narrow Lolo Trail. The trees were so thick that men had to hack a path for the horses. The cliffs were frighteningly steep. Lewis described a horse that fell over "and roled with his load … into the Creek. we all expected that the horse was killed but … he arose to his feet & appeared to be but little injured."

▲ When the explorers first saw the gigantic snow-capped Rocky Mountains, could they imagine themselves surviving a trip to the other side? The explorers crossed the mountains through the Bitterroot **Range.** This picture was painted by James Lanman.

THE FIELD BROTHERS
Reuben and Joseph Field were among the first men to join the Lewis and Clark **expedition.** Lewis described the brothers as "two of the most active and enterprising young men who accompanied us … engaged in all the most dangerous and difficult scenes of the voyage."

THE CONTINENTAL DIVIDE
In the Rocky Mountains, the explorers crossed the Continental Divide. To the west of the divide, rivers flow into the Pacific Ocean. To the east, rivers flow into the Atlantic Ocean, Gulf of Mexico, and Arctic Ocean.

THE OTHER SIDE

Just when the drenched, starving group felt they could stand no more, the first of them stumbled into a village of Nez Perce Indians by a stream of the Clearwater River. By September 22, all the explorers had made it through the mountains.

The friendly Nez Perce offered them salmon and berries, and the explorers stuffed themselves. In a few days, everyone was deathly sick. Perhaps they got sick from spoiled fish, or maybe it was just a change in diet. But it took the corps a few weeks to recover their strength.

The Nez Perce helped them make five canoes for their journey down the Clearwater River, the Snake River, the Columbia River, and to the Pacific Ocean. The corps usually made canoes by hollowing logs with axes. The Nez Perce taught them a quicker way: burning out the center of the logs. The corps would not need their horses until their return trip through the mountains. So they branded each horse with Lewis's name and left them all with the Nez Perce.

Back on the water

On October 7, the explorers set off for the last part of their westward trip. Unlike the beginning of the trip, the boats were now headed downstream. The group struggled through fifteen wild **rapids** in the first day alone. Boats tipped and supplies tumbled out. Sometimes the group had to **portage** the canoes.

Most days, the group stopped at villages belonging to the Chinook Indians to trade for food and gather information. One of the biggest problems in the Indian villages was fleas! Clark described them as "very . . . difficuelt to get rid of, . . . as the me[n] have not a Change of Clothes . . . they strip off their Clothes and kill the flees, dureing which time they remain nekid [naked]."

SEAMAN
Seaman was a large, black Newfoundland dog. Meriwether Lewis bought him in Pittsburgh less than a year before the **expedition** started. Seaman caught squirrels and geese, which the men ate. He was a strong swimmer and would dive underwater to force beavers to the surface. He also warned the corps when buffalo and grizzly bears were approaching. Along the way, American Indians offered three buffalo skins as a trade for Seaman. Lewis refused to trade.

▼ The Nez Perce remained friendly with the U.S. until the 1860s. By then the government had taken away much of their land. This is a picture of Chief Joseph. In the 1870s, he tried, unsuccessfully, to protect his people's land.

▼ When the Columbia River poured through wild rapids and waterfalls, the explorers sometimes carried their canoes around the rapids. Other times they tied elk-skin ropes to the canoes and lowered them over the rocks. The Chinook Indians were helpful in this work and in providing fish and dogs for the corps to eat.

MEETING AMERICAN INDIANS AUG 1805 TO JULY 1806
(Present-day locaations)
August 13, 1805 Shoshone near Three Forks, Montana
September 4 Salish (called Flathead) near Sula, Montana
September 20 Nez Perce near Weippe Prairie, Idaho
October 16 Wanapam in southern Washington
October 23 Chinook near Mount Hood, Oregon
December 12 Clatsop near Astoria, Oregon
January 6, 1806 Tillamook in northwest Oregon
April 1806 Walla Walla in southern Washington
July 1806 Blackfeet in northern Montana

Signs of the Pacific

As the corps traveled west, they could sense that the ocean was near. By October 27, they spotted sea otters in the water. Then the river water began rising and falling, an effect of the **tides** of the ocean. Some of the American Indians they saw were wearing sailor jackets and hats. They had probably gone to the Pacific coast where American and **British** ships were docked and traded furs for these clothes.

THE OCEAN IN VIEW

On November 7, 1805, William Clark wrote, "Ocian in View! O! the joy!" But he was wrong about the ocean. What he saw was Gray's Bay on the present-day border of Oregon and Washington. They were 20 miles (32 kilometers), and eight days, from the ocean.

CAPE DISAPPOINTMENT
Lewis walked to the coast to look for trading ships. He thought he could get food and supplies from a ship. Also, President Jefferson wanted the journals and maps sent back by ship. But Lewis found no ships. He must have agreed with the explorers who had named the spot Cape Disappointment. Clark carved on a tree there: "By Land from the U. States in 1804 & 1805."

THE REST OF THE TRIP WEST
August 13, 1805
Meet the Shoshone
September 1 to 21
Cross the Bitterroot
Range of the Rocky Mountains
September 20 Meet the Nez Perce
October 7 Set out on the Clearwater River to the Snake River
October 16 Reach the Columbia River
November 15 First sight of Pacific Ocean
December 7 Begin building Fort Clatsop
March 23, 1806 Begin the trip home

That last week was spent in the pouring rain. When the soaked explorers finally saw the Pacific on November 15, Clark simply wrote, "this I could plainly See would be the extent of our journey by water, as the waves were too high … for our canoes to proceed…." They were at present-day Baker Bay. They were still a few miles from the ocean, but could clearly see it. This is where they stopped.

The Corps of Discovery had crossed the continent! It had taken eighteen months. They never found a waterway that connected the Atlantic and Pacific oceans. Instead they proved that no such waterway exists.

▼ Clark heard about a beached whale on the coast and hoped to get some fresh whale **blubber** to eat. He, Sacagawea, and ten others traveled two days to the coast. By the time they arrived, the local Tillamook Indians had turned the whale into a skeleton.

Fort Clatsop

On December 7, the corps chose a site by a small river near present-day Astoria, Oregon. They named the camp Fort Clatsop after the local Clatsop Indians. On Christmas Eve, the corps moved in for a three-month stay. It rained all but twelve days. Fevers, colds, and fleas made the men miserable. Some men hunted elk, deer, beavers, and otters for their winter food, but the damp weather made the meat spoil. Some men camped by the ocean, where they boiled ocean water to make salt to flavor their food. Others kept busy making new pants and shirts and 258 pairs of elk-skin moccasins for the return trip. The clothes they brought with them were constantly damp and rotting away.

The Clatsop helped keep the corps alive with the fish and roots they collected. But by this time, the corps had few goods left to trade. Besides, American and **British** ships had been trading with the Clatsop for years.
The tired, sickly explorers did not interest them.

▼ The beached whale was near the Tillamook village of Necost. Today the site is Ecola State Park in Oregon. Clark traded with the Tillamook for 300 pounds of blubber and a few gallons of oil.

▲ This is Fort Clatsop National Memorial in Astoria, Oregon. When the corps built their camp, it had two log buildings. One of the buildings included two rooms for Lewis and Clark and one for Sacagawea, Charbonneau, and their child. The rest of the men shared the other building's rooms.

HEADING FOR HOME

The Corps of Discovery had met their goal. They shared an adventure beyond their wildest dreams. They accomplished something big for themselves and their country. But now they were over 4,000 miles (6,400 kilometers) from their homes and families.

On March 23, the explorers started for home. They had been gone nearly two years. Clark studied his maps and chose a route that cut 600 miles (965 kilometers) off the trip. Almost no supplies were left. At every stop, the corps tried to get food and horses from the American Indians. Lewis used his medicine and knowledge of healing to trade for salmon, dogs, and roots. The explorers traveled in canoes from the Columbia River to the Snake River. Then they sold their canoes and traveled with their horses.

By early May, the corps found the Nez Perce and picked up the horses they had left with them. Now they had more than 60 horses. By June 24, much of the snow had melted in the Rockies, and the corps headed up the Lolo Trail.

▶ Clark traveled down the Yellowstone River with 22 people, including Sacagawea and Pomp. He drew maps and sketched animals along the way. In the background is a rock formation near present-day Billings, Montana. Clark named it Pompy's Tower in honor of Pomp.

SPREADING THE NEWS

People of the United States were hungry for news about the corps. Yet more than a year went by with no word. Everyone assumed the entire corps was lost or dead. In the fall of 1806, Lewis finally sent a letter to a newspaper in Frankfort, Kentucky. He said there was no complete water route across the continent, but there was a land and water route. By November, stories of the **expedition** appeared in newspapers throughout the United States.

On July 25, 1806, Clark carved his name on the rock formation that he called Pompy's Tower. Today visitors can still see Clark's name under a piece of shatterproof glass. The corps carved their names on other rocks and trees, but those names seem to have disappeared.

THE ONLY AMERICAN INDIANS KILLED

On July 26, Lewis and three explorers met eight members of the Blackfeet tribe near the Marias River. The next morning, the Blackfeet took guns and rifles from the corps. Reuben Field stabbed one of the Blackfeet. When the Indians tried to run off with his horses, Lewis shot and killed another Blackfeet.

Splitting up

Once through the mountains, Lewis and Clark made a risky decision. To gather more information, they split up the group. They picked a meeting place with the hope that they would see each other again. Sure enough, on August 12, the corps reunited where the Yellowstone River meets the Missouri River, near present-day Williston, South Dakota.

On August 14, the corps arrived at the Mandan and Hidatsa villages. One member, John Colter, decided to stay there and become a fur **trader.** Charbonneau decided to stay, too. Lewis and Clark paid him $500 for his services. (Today that is worth $7,200.) Sacagawea and her son stayed with Charbonneau, though she was paid nothing. Lewis and Clark convinced Chief Big White to come to Washington to meet President Jefferson. Five members of Big White's family joined him.

SHARING THE ADVENTURE

After two years, four months, and ten days of traveling more than 7,000 miles (11,200 kilometers) the Corps of Discovery paddled up the Mississippi River in St. Louis. The date was September 23, 1806. From the banks of the river, crowds cheered and waved.

The leaders of St. Louis threw an elegant ball for Lewis and Clark. Three days later, the captains left St. Louis for Washington, D.C. Towns along the way held celebrations for the heroes. Adventure lovers, business leaders, and scientists applauded the captains. They had mapped the newest part of the United States, started friendships with American Indians, and discovered 122 animals and 178 plants that were new to science.

The members of the corps went their separate ways. Each was given a grant of land and money for his services. They earned between $166 and $250. That is worth $2,400 to $3,600 today. Some members became farmers. Some became guides for others who wanted to head to the West.

The lives of Lewis and Clark
Jefferson appointed Meriwether Lewis as governor of Upper Louisiana **Territory,** but Lewis suffered from malaria caught on the trip and the illness discouraged him. This may have led to his suicide on October 9, 1809, at the age of 35. William Clark had a more successful career. One of his jobs was to be in charge of Indian affairs. He continued some of the friendships with tribes he had met on the **expedition.** Unfortunately, the American Indians suffered more and more as Americans wanted to take over their western land. By 1890, most of the American Indians who survived were living on **reservations.** William Clark married twice and had five children. He died in 1838 at the age of 69.

► Lewis and Big White went directly to Washington, D.C., to meet the president. Clark first went to Virginia to see his family and the woman that he would soon marry. The people of Washington gave the men a hero's welcome.

▲ This painting by Charles Deas is called *Mountain Man of the American West.* Mountain men were guides who took explorers and settlers along rugged trails through the mountains. After the Lewis and Clark expedition, many other United States citizens decided to head west.

WHO CLAIMS OREGON

1800 Oregon stretches from Alaska to California. Russia, Spain, Great Britain, and U.S. claim parts of the area.

1819 Spain gives up land north of California.

1824 and 1825 Russia gives up land south of present-day British Columbia, Canada. Citizens of the U.S. and Great Britain live in Oregon.

1846 present border between the United States and Canada (Britain) is set.

SACAGAWEA AND FAMILY

In 1810, Sacagawea, Charbonneau, and six-year-old Pomp traveled from their Hidatsa village to visit Clark in St. Louis.

Sacagawea and Charbonneau stayed for a few months. Clark offered to keep Pomp and send him to school. Pomp played the violin and studied languages. He knew seven languages: Hidatsa, Shoshone, English, French, Latin, Greek, and Italian. As an adult, he was an explorer and mountain guide. He died in 1866 at the age of 61.

Sacagawea died in 1812 at around age 22. She had just given birth to a daughter, named Lizette. Charbonneau died in 1839 at around the age of 80.

◄ Chief Big White, shown here in the center, wearing American clothes, stayed in Washington for three years. Then the president sent him back to his Mandan village with a fur trading company. At least 120 armed men traveled with the chief to make sure he arrived safely.

HISTORICAL MAP OF THE UNITED STATES

ALASKA

CANADA

Aleutian Islands

The Lewis and Clark **expedition** traveled along the Missouri River to the Rocky Mountains. It crossed the mountains in the Bitterroot **Range.** From there, it traveled by rivers to the Pacific Ocean. The westward trip took one year, six months, and one day, including an almost four-month winter stop at Fort Mandan. The return route was shorter by about 600 miles (965 kilometers) and took six months. The entire trip covered about 7,700 miles (12,390 kilometers).

WASHINGTON
Seattle
Astoria
Fort Clatsop
Columbia River
Tillamook Bay
Portland

R O C K

Milk River
Lewis & Clark
Lewis' return
Great Falls Missouri River
MONTANA
Clark's return
Pompy's Tower
Yellowstone River

OREGON COUNTRY
BITTERROOT MOUNTAINS
IDAHO
Snake River
Fort Hall

OREGON
CONTINENTAL DIVIDE
WYOMING

Sacramento
San Francisco

NEVADA
Salt Lake City
UTAH
COLORADO

M O U N T A I N S

CALIFORNIA
SPANISH MEXICO
ARIZONA
Santa Fe

Los Angeles
Colorado River
NEW MEXICO

El Paso

PACIFIC OCEAN

MEXICO

Kauai
Oahu
Maui
Hawaii
HAWAIIAN ISLANDS

N
W   E
S

〜 Route of Lewis and Clark
〜 River

0	250	500 miles
0	400	800 kilometers

Hudson Bay

C A N A D A

Lake Superior

MINNESOTA

NORTH DAKOTA

⑤ Fort Mandan

SOUTH DAKOTA

Lewis & Clark

④

③

②

NEBRASKA

① Council Bluffs

Missouri River

WISCONSIN

Lake Michigan

IOWA

Chicago

Mississippi River

ILLINOIS

INDIANA

Lake Huron

MICHIGAN

Lake Erie

Lake Ontario

St. Lawrence

MAINE

VERMONT

NEW HAMPSHIRE

MASSACHUSETTS

Boston

NEW YORK

RHODE ISLAND

CONNECTICUT

Hudson River

New York City

Delaware River

NEW JERSEY

Philadelphia

DELAWARE

MARYLAND

Washington, D.C.

ATLANTIC OCEAN

PENNSYLVANIA

Pittsburgh

OHIO

WEST VIRGINIA

VIRGINIA

James River

KANSAS

Independence

Lewis & Clark

St. Louis

Ohio River

MISSOURI

UNITED STATES

KENTUCKY

TENNESSEE

APPALACHIAN MOUNTAINS

NORTH CAROLINA

LOUISIANA PURCHASE

OKLAHOMA

Fort Smith

Arkansas River

Memphis

Mississippi River

SOUTH CAROLINA

Charleston

Atlanta

GEORGIA

Savannah

ARKANSAS

MISSISSIPPI

ALABAMA

TEXAS

LOUISIANA

New Orleans

SPANISH FLORIDA

FLORIDA

Rio Grande River

GULF OF MEXICO

CARIBBEAN SEA

Sites of major meetings with American Indians:

1. Council Bluffs, August 3, 1804. Meeting with Missouri and Oto Indians.

2. Calumnet Bluff, August 30–31, 1804. Held council with Yankton Sioux.

3. Bad River, September 25, 1804. Held council with Teton Sioux.

4. Arikara campsite, October 12, 1804. Held council with Arikaras.

5. Mandan and Hidatsa villages, October 27, 1804–April 7, 1805. Spent winter with Mandan and Hidatsa Indians.

6. With the Shoshones, August 13–30, 1805.

7. Canoe campsite, September 24–October 7, 1805. Camp near Nez Perce Indians.

8. Fort Clatsop, December 7, 1805–March 23, 1806

GLOSSARY

bellows tool that makes a strong blast of air by pressing two handles together. It is used to make a fire stronger.

blubber layer of fat below a whale's skin

border dividing line between two countries

British people or things of England or Great Britain. In 1707, England, Scotland, and Wales joined to form Great Britain. *Britain* is another term for Great Britain.

expedition journey made for a specific purpose, such as exploring

fork place where a river divides into two branches. One of the branches is also called a fork.

French and Indian War (1754 to 1763) war fought in North America between the British and the French. American Indians fought on both sides. As a result of the war, Britain gained France's land east of the Mississippi River, except New Orleans.

headwaters source or upper part of a river

keelboat boat with a square sail designed for shallow rivers. A keelboat can carry heavy loads.

mill building where things are made by machines, such as a cloth mill

pirogue long, narrow boat similar to a canoe

plantation large farm where crops such as cotton and tobacco are grown

port place where ships and boats can load and unload

portage carry boats and supplies between two waterways

rapids part of a river where water quickly rushes over rocks

range row or line of mountains

reservation area of land set aside by the government for American Indians to live on

settlement group of buildings, and the people living in them

slave person who is owned by another person and is made to work for that person

territory area of the United States that is not yet organized as a state

tide rise and fall of the ocean about every twelve hours, caused by the pull of the Moon and the Sun

trader person who purchases things by exchanging one kind of goods for another

trading post place where people trade goods with people who live in the area. For example, a fur trader exchanges animal furs for other goods.

trapper person who catches animals in order to kill them and sell their fur

translate change from one language to another

BOOKS TO READ

Faber, Harold. *Lewis and Clark from Ocean to Ocean.* New York: Benchmark Books/Marshall Cavendish, 2002.

Osgood, Ernest S. and Donald Jackson. *The Lewis and Clark Expedition's Newfoundland Dog.* Great Falls, MT: The Lewis and Clark Heritage Foundation, 1986.

Gunderson, Mary. *Cooking on the Lewis and Clark Expedition.* Mankato, Minn.: Capstone Press, 2000.

Thorp, Daniel B. *An American Journey Lewis & Clark.* New York: Michael Freidman Publishing Group, Inc., 1998.

TIMELINE OF EVENTS IN THIS BOOK

1778 Great Britain's James Cook explores the Pacific coast near Canada

1792 American Robert Gray discovers the Columbia River in Oregon

1800 Britain's Alexander Mackenzie travels across Canada to the Pacific Ocean

March 4, 1801 Thomas Jefferson becomes the third U.S. President

May 2, 1803 The United States doubles in size when it signs the Louisiana Purchase treaty with France

May 14, 1804 The Lewis and Clark **expedition** leaves Camp Dubois

October 24 Corps arrives at Mandan and Hidatsa villages for the winter

November 4 Charbonneau and Sacagawea join the expedition

April 7, 1805 Corps leaves Fort Mandan

May 26 Lewis first sees the Rocky Mountains

June 22 Corps begins **portage** of the Great Falls

July 4 Corps completes portage of the Great Falls

August 13 Corps meets the Shoshone

September 1 to 21 Corps crosses the Bitterroot **Range** of the Rocky Mountains

September 20 Corps meets the Nez Perce

October 7 Corps sets out on the Clearwater River to the Snake River

October 16 Corps reaches the Columbia River

November 15 Corps first sees the Pacific Ocean

December 7 Corps begins building Fort Clatsop

March 23, 1806 The trip home begins

May 7 Corps returns to the Nez Perce and pick up most of its horses

June 24 Corps begins crossing the Rocky Mountains

July 3 Corps splits up to explore

July 25 Clark carves his name on Pompy's Tower

July 27 Two Blackfeet are killed by Lewis's group

August 12 All groups reunite

August 14 Sacagawea, Charbonneau, and Pomp say goodbye to the corps at the Mandan and Hidatsa villages

September 23, 1806 Expedition ends at St. Louis

PLACES TO VISIT

Lewis and Clark National Historic Trail
Interpretive Center
4201 Giant Springs Road
P.O. Box 1806
Great Falls, MT 59403
Telephone: (406) 727-8733

Sacagawea State Park and Interpretive
Center
2503 Sacagawea Park Road
Pasco, WA 99301
Telephone: (509) 545-2361

Lewis and Clark National Historical Trail
1709 Jackson St.,
Omaha, NE 68102
Telephone: (402) 514 9311

Knife River Indian Villages National
Historic Site
P.O. Box 9
564 County Road 37
Stanton, ND 58571
Telephone: (701) 745-3309

Fort Clatsop National Memorial
92342 Fort Clatsop Road
Astoria, OR 97103
Telephone: (503) 861-2471

INDEX